THIS CANDLEWICK BIOGRAPHY BELONGS TO:

One Beetle Too Many

The Extraordinary Adventures of Charles Darwin

Kathryn Lasky

illustrated by Matthew Trueman

Candlewick Press

In celebration of children,
whose boundless curiosity gives them
a right to know their history on Earth

K. L.

To my MinaBug

M. T.

This book is entirely based on facts about the life of Charles Darwin, drawn from the wide array of sources available. It should be noted, however, that the event that inspired the book's title, *One Beetle Too Many,* occurred somewhat later in his life than might be inferred.

First edition in this format 2014

Library of Congress Catalog Card Number 2002071254

ISBN 978-0-7636-1436-2 (hardcover edition)
ISBN 978-0-7636-5821-2 (paperback edition)
ISBN 978-0-7636-6842-6 (reformatted hardcover edition)
ISBN 978-0-7636-6843-3 (reformatted paperback edition)

13 14 15 16 17 18 SWT 10 9 8 7 6 5 4 3 2 1
Printed in Dongguan, Guangdong, China

This book was typeset in Berkeley Old Style.
The illustrations were done in graphite pencil, acrylic ink and watercolor, gouache, colored pencil, acrylic, and collaged with paper, string, weeds, and wildflowers.

Candlewick Press
99 Dover Street
Somerville, Massachusetts 02144

visit us at www.candlewick.com

TABLE OF CONTENTS

CHAPTER ONE

ONE BEETLE TOO MANY

No one ever said "Don't touch!" in the house where Charles Darwin grew up. And there was so much to touch, because the Darwin household was a scramble of children, odd pets, and wonderful books.

Charles's mother, Susannah Darwin, raised fancy pigeons known for their beauty and tameness. Dr. Robert Darwin, Charles's father, was an immense man who weighed 336 pounds. He would drive all over the countryside to visit his patients in a single-seat carriage stuffed with snacks. When he returned from a long day of house calls, his six children would swirl about the huge man like little moons orbiting Jupiter.

Charles was happiest when he was out alone collecting. He especially liked to collect beetles. He found them under the bark of trees, in rotten logs, between the cracks of old stone walls, and even in puddles and ponds. Looking through his magnifying glass, he would wonder why the diving beetle had a smooth back and the whirligig beetle that spun in circles on the pond's surface had no grooves at all. Why would one beetle's legs be hairy and another's nearly bare?

As he grew up, he continued to collect specimens. Once, out on a beetling expedition, he found under the bark of a tree two beetles he had never seen before. Within seconds a third strange beetle crawled out, and Charles, lacking a free hand, quickly popped one beetle into his mouth and scooped up the third one. Then he ran for his collecting bottle.

When Charles was eight, his mother died, and at age nine he was sent away to boarding school. But as keen as his powers of observation were, Charles Darwin was not a good student. He hated Latin and Greek and all the subjects that a young scholar was supposed to learn. He still loved bugs and worms and creatures of the wild.

Charles learned the names of everything he collected, for to know the names of these things was important, and it might be the one time when adults would actually listen to a child speak. Charles could be both liked and admired when he talked about his collections.

When his brother, Erasmus, returned from the university on holidays, the two would set up a chemistry laboratory for experiments. They fitted out a garden shed behind the house with test tubes and beakers, blowpipes and evaporating dishes, burners and stoppers. They made laughing gas and turned sixpences into silver by dissolving them in chemical solutions. Explosions were their favorite things—these were much more fun than Latin and Greek. Soon Charles was nicknamed Gas because of his activities in the laboratory. His father, however, was the one who really exploded—over Charles's poor grades in school. He once told Charles, "You . . . will be a disgrace to yourself and all your family!"

CHAPTER TWO

ANATOMY, THEOLOGY, AND BOTANY

Charles's father felt that what the "poor student" needed was more serious study farther away from home. So when Charles was just sixteen, his father sent him to study medicine at the University of Edinburgh in Scotland. He hated it. He found anatomy class disgusting, and he once rushed out of an operating room, unable to stand the sight of blood.

Charles joined a science club. And although his teachers gave him low grades, his fellow students in the club knew that Charles was a born naturalist and elected him to its special council. Still, his grades were poor, and even his younger sister wrote to correct his spelling in letters from home: "*Altogether* has only one *l*, not *alltogether,* as you spelt it in your letter to Papa . . . dear Charley."

Papa was very irritated. There was only one profession for a lazy, mediocre student like Charles, Dr. Darwin decided—the clergy. So Charles was sent to the University of Cambridge to study theology and become a cleric.

Charles hated theology as much as he hated anatomy and the operating room. It was less bloody—that was the only good thing he could say about it. Charles spent as little time as possible on his studies.

He joined a foxhunting club and the Glutton Club, and when not hunting or eating, he enjoyed music, drinking, and going to parties. Still, his first love was collecting, and he became close friends at Cambridge with a professor of botany named John Henslow. Together they took long walks, studied nature, and, of course, went beetling and plant collecting. On one such trip Charles spotted, across a muddy ditch, a rare plant that he knew Henslow very much wanted. Charles tried to pole-vault himself over the ditch but instead wound up clinging to the top of the pole until he finally splashed down into the muck. Henslow thought Charles would make a much better scientist than clergyman. He told him so. But Charles was afraid to go against his father's wishes.

Charles passed all of his courses. For a summer holiday he went to Wales to study rocks. Then he planned to go partridge shooting. On the night before the partridge shoot, a fat envelope arrived. Inside was a letter from his friend Henslow. It was to change his life forever.

CHAPTER THREE

THE VOYAGE OF A LIFETIME BEGINS

He was told that it was something no clergyman should do. That it was a wild scheme. That the boat was unsafe. That the voyage would be useless. That this was a most unsuitable occupation and would ruin his character. And if all that were not enough, he would surely get horribly seasick and furthermore the natives would probably eat him!

In spite of these objections from his father and sisters and aunts and uncles, Charles still wanted to go. He had been recommended by Henslow to serve as a naturalist aboard a naval vessel that was to survey the southern coasts of South America under the command of Captain Robert Fitzroy. The British knew very little about South America. British scientists, who for most of their lives had been confined to their tiny island nation, found the notion of exploring an entire continent with deserts and jungles and volcanic mountain ranges very exciting. The thought to Charles was irresistible—he would see flowers, animals, birds, and insects that could not be seen elsewhere. And, for Henslow, Charles Darwin was the man for the job as he had, in Henslow's words, "zeal" and "spirit." He was twenty-two years old.

Fitzroy, at twenty-six, was already considered one of England's finest sailing captains. He had spent most of his life at sea, and his favorite book to read on his travels was the Bible. Over and over he read the stories of the Creation, and while the world beyond his ship constantly changed, those comforting stories did not. Fitzroy was also a scientist, however, and had done excellent work in the field of astronomy and meteorology, the study of weather. He was devoted to the Bible, to science, and to the British navy. He had a particular fascination with the flood of Noah's time, for here his three interests—weather, sailing, and the Bible—came together in perfect harmony. Fitzroy, like Darwin, was full of questions and enthusiasm. Although they had never met before, the captain and the collector seemed in many ways a perfect match. Seasickness or not, stubborn father or not, clergyman or not, Charles just had to go. Finally his father agreed.

On December 27, 1831, the *Beagle* hoisted its anchor and set sail. The *Beagle* was a small ship, a brigantine, ninety feet long by twenty-four feet wide. Charles's tiny cabin was in the rear, or stern, of the boat, under the poop deck. In fact, the only way that Charles could stretch out fully in his hammock was by removing a drawer in the wall so his feet could slide in. All other space was for his collections and his laboratory with its scientific equipment.

Charles was sick almost from the start, but he never lost his excitement about the adventure that lay before him. As gales blew, Charles swung violently in his hammock, too weak to wonder and not steady enough to wander. He could only stagger above deck to vomit over the rail into the tossing sea. He could eat nothing but raisins for days.

The *Beagle's* first stop was St. Jago, in the Cape Verde Islands. Charles was thrilled to be on dry land. Exploring St. Jago was the first time that he had ever seen a volcanic island. When he discovered rock cliffs embedded with seashells, he was simply astonished, as he realized that what was now dry land had once lain at the bottom of the sea. What was even more astounding for Darwin was his realization of just how much time this process must have taken. How long would it have taken this island to stagger up from the ocean's depths and break through the surface of the sea? For the cliffs to climb from the water? For the lava ridges to rise above sea level? How long would it have taken them to become part of dry land? Darwin began to think in terms of millions of years and not just thousands.

When Charles was not hammering with his geology tools or gathering samples of rock, he was often flat on his belly, observing the creatures of the island's tidal pools. More than once he was squirted in the face by an octopus as he peered closely to observe the strange "blushes" by which the creature changed color from brownish purple

to yellowish green to a shade Charles called French gray. Charles finally figured out that the octopus changed its color in relation to the ground over which it swam. He took one back to the ship in a jar, and from his hammock he watched the tentacled creature turn phosphorescent at night, glowing in the darkness of the tiny cabin like an eight-legged night-light.

While Charles was scrambling over the rocky outcrops or skimming the surrounding waters with his collecting nets, Fitzroy was setting up an observatory on the island and taking precise measurements of the stars by which he navigated his ship. One man kept his eyes firmly fixed on Earth; the other looked toward the sky.

The ship sailed on, and when the *Beagle* crossed the equator, the crew, following an ancient local ritual, seized Charles, shaved him, doused him with buckets of water, lathered him with pitch and paint, and dumped him into a large tub of water. Charles was a good sport about it.

CHAPTER FOUR

BUTTERFLIES AND GAUCHOS

By February 1832 the sturdy *Beagle* had crossed the Atlantic and arrived in Brazil. Charles was enraptured as immense blue morpho butterflies fluttered silently around him, monstrous anthills rose like giant cones from the rain forest floor, and brilliant birds—toucans, green parrots, and cockatiels—swooped in glittering flights through the canopy. He collected specimens for his jars—an insect that looked like a stick of dry wood, a moth that could disguise itself as a scorpion, a beetle that could change its colors to match those of a poisonous fruit.

In the jungles and rain forest, there was a frightening law: prey or be preyed upon. Darwin observed a long battle between a wasp and a spider, and he watched the fantastic marches of army ants. The ants mowed down anything in their path. Snakes, spiders, lizards, and chameleons attempted to flee at the first sign of an army on the march. But often they failed as the ants, with exact timing, would first break their lines into a circle and then

rush in upon their victims. Swarming over a lizard hundreds of times the size of a single ant, they could devour it within an hour.

Charles also saw a brutality in humans that was easily as bad as the wars between the species of the rain forest. It was not wasp against spider or ant against lizard but human against human. It was slavery.

Staying on Brazilian plantations, he encountered firsthand the cruelty of masters to slaves. He wrote, "I thank God I shall never again visit a slave country. . . . I have seen a little boy, six or seven years old, struck thrice with a horsewhip (before I could interfere)

on his naked head, for having handed me a glass of water not quite clean."

Fitzroy felt differently about slavery. He felt that it was justifiable. He had seen more of the world than Darwin; perhaps he was used to it. But Darwin knew that, no matter how far he traveled, he would never get used to seeing human beings bought and sold and cruelly treated. It was evil, and he told Fitzroy so. The captain, who had a fierce temper, did not like to be contradicted. The crew had nicknamed him Hot Coffee because he often boiled over when he was angry. He was furious now. This was Darwin and Fitzroy's first big argument.

Darwin was beginning to realize that he and Fitzroy were not the perfect match. And the test was about to come as they sailed south from Brazil along the eastern coast of Argentina toward the tip of the continent of South America, a region called Patagonia.

At Punta Alta, a gravelly beach on the coast of Bahía Blanca, in Argentina, Darwin made one of his greatest discoveries. Near the base of a cliff, he spotted some large fossilized bones emerging from the beach rubble—a tusk, a claw turned to stone, a huge carapace—unlike any bones he had ever seen. They were immense. He and an assistant set to work with a pickax. The bones were encased in a mixture of red mud, gravel, and seashells. The seashells were not those of extinct creatures but instead identical to those he saw living on the beaches and in the shallow waters. Still, the shells had their origins in prehistoric times. The clams had not died out but continued to live to the very day that Darwin stood on that beach. Yet the strange bones that he had uncovered clearly belonged to creatures that no longer existed. Why had these animals died out when the clams had not?

Darwin realized that his eyes were perhaps the first human eyes to have ever seen these bones. In all, there were fragments from at least six different animals. The jawbone of one looked somewhat like that of a tree sloth he had seen in the rain forest, but this one was nearly eight times larger than its modern relative. The bones of

another were similar to those of the burrowing armadillo. Could there be a relationship between the living life forms and the extinct ones? Could one have descended from the other? Would this mean that animals had not always been the same but were constantly changing over the history of the earth? Maybe creation was not a weeklong event, as described in the Bible, but a much longer process that was, in fact, still happening. Darwin stood on that beach at Punta Alta, contemplating the very exciting notion that all living things were still changing, or evolving.

Fitzroy was not impressed. Darwin's collecting had begun to make him nervous. He felt that Darwin was littering the *Beagle's* scrubbed decks with "rubbish." To Darwin the bones were fascinating—and puzzling. They filled Darwin with questions: where were all these animals during the flood? There was no mention of such beasts on Noah's ark. Indeed, how would such huge creatures have fitted into the ark? He asked Fitzroy this question.

Fitzroy answered that not all animals had been able to get aboard the ark. Some, such as the ones Darwin found, had, in fact, drowned. But Darwin did not believe that the ark had ever floated where these animal bones were found. Since clams are the kinds of creatures that live in an estuary, Darwin believed that this land had perhaps been mudflats, which would not have been swept away in a gigantic flood. This was Darwin's second big argument with Fitzroy.

Through summer and winter the *Beagle* sailed on, surveying the coast of South America. Darwin himself took a break from the sailing—and perhaps from his arguments with Fitzroy—and traveled on land to the Pampas, a region of plains extending westward across Argentina. He spent many weeks riding the Pampas with horsemen known as *gauchos.*

Darwin loved riding with the *gauchos,* camping out, eating the armadillos they roasted over the fires and then settling back to listen to their stories. The *gauchos* had creation stories of their own and told how the stars were made from old Indians who hunted across a field, the Milky Way, for the elusive ostriches in the heavens.

After four months of exploring ashore, Darwin rejoined the *Beagle* at the end of 1833.

CHAPTER FIVE
SEASHELLS ON MOUNTAINTOPS

As they sailed on, Darwin's collection grew. There were spiders that spun webs like sails; snakes preserved in alcohol; *bolas,* a kind of slingshot the *gauchos* used to bring down prey; seeds with wings; skins of birds; and bones of prehistoric animals. At Port Desire, near the tip of South America, Darwin was enjoying a delicious bird for dinner with his shipmates when suddenly he peered closely at the bone in his hand—good grief! Could this be the very rare bird the *gauchos* had told him about? Could he be devouring a nearly extinct bird? He jumped up from the table and raced to the galley, where he was able to save the bones and the feathers before the cook tossed them overboard. From these remnants, a nearly perfect specimen was put together that gave many clues to the changes in ostriches over time. This species had never been known before. Scientists back in England named it *Rhea darwinii* after Darwin.

As the *Beagle* rounded the tip of South America and sailed northward up the western coast of the continent, Darwin looked at the towering cordillera of the Andes mountains that gleamed with white crests and tried to imagine how on earth they ever got so high.

For Fitzroy, the answer was simple. The mountains were the works of almighty God, and they had always been there. Darwin, too, believed that they were the works of a Creator, but he did not believe that the mountains had always looked the way they did when they were first created. He soon encountered the proof of his belief.

In Valdivia, a small settlement up a river, Charles had just stretched out on the ground to rest when suddenly the earth began to shiver, then shake violently. He wrote in a letter home, "It came on suddenly and lasted two minutes. . . . There was no difficulty in standing upright but the motion made me giddy." It was, he said, like "skating on very thin ice." Charles Darwin was experiencing his first earthquake, and all the questions that he had encountered in the months earlier began to be answered. It was as if pieces of a puzzle were literally falling into place before his eyes.

After the quake, Charles raced into the town, where he saw streets gone askew and houses turned lopsided. Great cracks split the earth, and huge chunks had dropped off the sides of cliffs, while fields and beaches buckled up. During the earthquake in Valdivia, Charles Darwin had seen with his own eyes that land can change shape within the space of minutes.

Charles set out on horseback to explore the Andes. When he reached 13,000 feet above sea level, he found evidence that confirmed his sense of the changing nature of the earth. At that elevation, Darwin spied many fossilized seashells. Although on St. Jago he had seen seashells on the rock cliffs, those cliffs had risen straight up from the sea. But this was no island, and here the sea was miles and miles away. Seashells on mountaintops? The idea seemed ridiculous. Had the sea at one time reached this high? Or had the mountains first formed out of the sea and been pushed up over time through earthquakes?

When Darwin encountered a white petrified forest of pine trees, he found more fossil shells scattered on the ground. Perhaps, he speculated, these mountains first formed out of the sea as small, wooded islands. Maybe, as the mountains rose higher over millions of years, the cold killed the trees, leaving them to petrify in the dry, frigid air—a ghost forest from a dim, nearly unimaginable past.

In the aftermath of the Valdivian earthquake, Charles could not help but point out to Fitzroy the change in the actual level of the surrounding land. It was higher by a few feet than it had been before. Was this not proof that the earth, that mountains, could rise from the sea?

Even though Darwin believed in change, that did not mean that he did not believe in God or a Creator. He would later write in reply to a question about his religion, "I do not believe in the Bible as divine revelation and therefore not in Jesus Christ as the Son of God." But he did believe in a Creator who had "originally breathed" life into the earliest forms of living things.

CHAPTER SIX
GALÁPAGOS ISLANDS

For almost four years the *Beagle* had been surveying the South American coasts, and it was time to move on. Now the *Beagle* set out for the Galápagos Islands, located in the Pacific along the equator, six hundred miles west of South America.

In these small islands Darwin encountered other mysteries and puzzles—changes in animals over long periods of time. The animals became different just as the earth had. What Darwin saw in the Galápagos was to influence his thinking more than anything else he saw during the entire five years of the *Beagle*'s voyage. But he did not realize it at the time. Indeed, Darwin unwittingly ate his way through many of the most important animal specimens.

Charles Darwin noticed in the Galápagos that the same type of bird or tortoise or plant varied ever so slightly from one island to the next, even though the environmental conditions of the islands were similar. For example, the finches on one island might have stubby beaks, while those on another had slender ones. In all, he found thirteen different kinds of finches, each with a different-sized and -shaped beak. The differences he was seeing on these small islands and the observations he recorded did not form a picture or pattern in his mind until long after he was back in England.

From the Galápagos, the *Beagle* crossed the Pacific to New Zealand, Australia, and around Africa's Cape of Good Hope, then home, to England. All the time, Charles was collecting, observing, and wondering.

CHAPTER SEVEN

THE IDEA THAT SCARED THE WORLD

On October 2, 1836, the *Beagle* reached England. She had been gone for five long years. Charles's sister wrote to him that his father realized that Charles would never be a church man but instead a scientist. Darwin returned to find that not only had his father finally accepted him as a first-rate naturalist, but scientists throughout England had been awaiting his return. The letters and collections he had sent back to Henslow by other English ships along the way had made his work well known. People wanted to see more and hear more from the famous naturalist Charles Darwin.

At this time, Darwin began to have some serious stomach problems. And very often when he thought or began to write about how species changed over time, his stomach problems would become worse. He could not, however, avoid thinking about what he had seen in the Galápagos—the patterns of life on these small islands and why the inhabitants varied from island to island was a picture that was finally becoming clearer.

Darwin reasoned that the living things on Earth changed to better fit with their environment. Although some changes, such as those caused by an earthquake, could happen quickly, others, such as the changes in the beaks of finches of the Galápagos, would take millions and millions of years.

Many people, like Fitzroy, preferred the story of Earth's formation as described in the Bible. This belief is called creationism. Creationism fitted with their ideas of order. Humans were part of an order created by God. This order, in which God was at the top and insects at the bottom, was sometimes called the "Great Chain of Being." It was very important that every creature, from beetles to children, know its place. And modesty meant that one must look up and not down when considering one's position in the chain.

ANNIE

By 1837 Darwin felt pretty sure that all creatures on Earth, including humans—in other words, all species—had not always been the way they were in the present, but in fact had descended from earlier, simpler forms of life. The species were not fixed; they had and would change again and again over time. The world was not ready for this idea, so Darwin began to keep secret notebooks on the mutability of species. In these notebooks he wrote down his thoughts about how humans and animals might have changed over time. He felt that people were so proud and so arrogant that they could not imagine an origin for themselves that was the same as for animals, that God would never have allowed people to be anything else but people.

In 1839 Charles married his cousin Emma Wedgwood. Emma's family was even richer than Charles's. They made the pottery called creamware, which was used by the royal family. Because of their wealth, Charles was able to devote all his time to studying and writing. He began a study of barnacles—he had collected a strange one in Chile. He wrote about volcanoes and coral reefs. He was very interested in such domestic animals as cattle and sheep and how they changed over time through selective breeding.

When the Darwins started having children, Charles began another notebook called "The Natural History of Babies." He wondered about when and why babies blinked and the meaning of a baby's first smiles. He even found his son's naughtiness fascinating, and when little Willy tried to hide something from his father, Darwin wrote that it "was natural acting and deceit." He preferred to record rather than punish such behavior.

In all, Charles and Emma would have ten children. It was a lively household, since the children were allowed the run of the house. As one visitor said, there was only one place where you could always be certain never to find a child—in the nursery.

The children would often climb up on the sofa in their father's study as he wrote, especially if they weren't feeling well. His shelves were filled with plants and jars containing earthworms and barnacles, beetles and spiders. There was much to look at, to touch and wonder about. Darwin would often break to tell them a story.

Darwin still had not written publicly about how species changed over time. This was an idea that truly scared the world. Not only was the world not ready to be told that people had not always been people, dogs dogs, or fleas fleas, neither was Emma. Charles's beliefs frightened her, and she worried that he had lost his faith in God. Charles, however, felt that his notions did not disprove God in the least but in fact made God more powerful. In one notebook, he had written that if species had changed over time, then who else but God could make things happen in such a marvelous way? And in another secret notebook, he wrote that we should praise God for this power.

Some people were not scared by such an idea. Darwin's close friends knew what he had been working on. Darwin's brother warned that if Charles did not write about the origin of species, someone would beat him to it.

That nearly happened. Charles began work on his book in the spring of 1856. A year later his old stomach illness flared up once more, worse than ever. He went to take a "water cure," a popular new treatment at that time. He would be scrubbed each morning in cold water. He would then take walks with cold-water compresses strapped to various parts of his body and return to soak his feet in some more water. It seemed to help. But he lost work time, and in 1858, when he still had much to write, he received a paper from Alfred Russel Wallace, a young naturalist. Wallace was on his track and had been asking the same questions. The men wrote a paper together, and then Darwin raced ahead with a book.

The book was called *The Origin of Species.* In it Darwin presented his theory of evolution and how all living things had changed gradually, over time, having descended from a few simpler, more ancient forms. He was not sure how this happened, but he speculated that it was through a process that he called natural selection.

Natural selection, unlike the artificial selection that farmers use to breed cattle or sheep or pigs, happened freely in nature, where males and females of a species were attracted to one another for the purpose of sexual reproduction.

Darwin further speculated that through this process certain characteristics were passed down, and therefore some animals might have advantages that others did not. Those with advantages would more likely survive in a particular environment. He called this idea "survival of the fittest."

On the day it was published, November 24, 1859, all 1,250 copies of *The Origin of Species* sold out. There was a storm of controversy surrounding the publication. Criticism came from all sorts of people, ranging from clergymen to other scientists who could not give up their notions of creation as described in the Bible. Darwin's friends stuck by him, however, and the most steadfast of these was Thomas Huxley, who was ecstatic over Darwin's theory of evolution. He quickly became known as Darwin's Bulldog.

However, clergymen continued to attack Darwin, and Darwin continued to let Huxley take on the challenge. He himself preferred to keep studying and observing the natural world. Would an insect-eating plant eat as many insects if dosed with chloroform? He tried it.

Another experiment proved somewhat frustrating. As Emma wrote to their son Leonard, by then grown up, "Father . . . has taken to training earthworms but does not make much progress as they can neither see nor hear."

There was absolutely nothing under the sun—from carnivorous plants to cows, from fossil bones to volcanoes, from pigeons to barnacles, from orchids to earthquakes—that did not absorb the mind of Charles Darwin. "I am," he wrote, "a complete millionaire in odd and curious facts."

Bibliography

Bowlby, John. *Charles Darwin: A New Life.* New York: W. W. Norton, 1990.

Darwin, Charles. *The Autobiography of Charles Darwin, 1809–1892.* Edited by Nora Barlow. New York: W. W. Norton, 1958.

———. *The Darwin Reader.* Edited by Mark Ridley. New York: W. W. Norton, 1987.

———. *The Descent of Man and Selection in Relation to Sex.* Princeton, NJ: Princeton University Press, 1981.

———. *The Illustrated Origin of Species.* Abridged and introduced by Richard E. Leakey. New York: Hill and Wang, 1979.

———. *The Origin of Species.* With an introduction by L. Harrison Matthews. London: Dent, 1972.

———. *The Voyage of Charles Darwin.* Selected by Christopher Ralling. New York: Ariel Books, 1978.

———. *The Voyage of the* Beagle. Annotated and with an introduction by Leonard Engel. New York: Anchor Books, 1962.

Desmond, Adrian, and James Moore. *Darwin: The Life of a Tormented Evolutionist.* New York: Warner Books, 1991.

Gillespie, Neal C. *Charles Darwin and the Problem of Creation.* Chicago: University of Chicago Press, 1979.

Gould, Stephen Jay. *The Panda's Thumb.* New York: W. W. Norton, 1980.

Marks, Richard Lee. *Three Men of the* Beagle. New York: Alfred A. Knopf, 1991.

Moorehead, Alan. *Darwin and the* Beagle. New York: Harper and Row, 1969.

AUTHOR'S NOTE

In many ways, I see this book as a celebration of human imagination. The role of imagination in science is greatly underrated. This is not to undermine the authority of science or to say that imagination is at odds with valid methods of scientific inquiry. It merely is an acknowledgment that it takes a lot of imagination just to observe, begin to gain insight, and hypothesize.

Darwin had it all, including the doggedness to study a subject like barnacles for nearly a decade. This was a tedious job that led him to remark, "I hate a Barnacle as no man ever did before, not even a sailor on a slow moving ship." But, as with so many of the organisms he collected or grew, he studied them to see how one tiny barnacle compared to others and to discover the relationships between various kinds and classes of barnacles.

—Kathryn Lasky

Illustrator's Note

Wandering around with my nose in the grass while collecting the weeds, wildflowers, and herbs for these pictures made me feel a little bit like Charles Darwin. Then concocting different ways to sneak them into paintings was similar to a secret science experiment. Working on this book reminded me that when closely observed, every little plant is strange and mysterious.

–Matthew Trueman

INDEX

Kathryn Lasky is the author of numerous books of fiction and nonfiction, including *Sugaring Time*, a Newbery Honor Book; *A Voice of Her Own: The Story of Phillis Wheatley, Slave Poet*; *Interrupted Journey: Saving Endangered Sea Turtles*; *John Muir: America's First Environmentalist*; and *Vision of Beauty: The Story of Sarah Breedlove Walker*. About *One Beetle Too Many*, she says, "Many people have argued over Charles Darwin's ideas. His careful observations of nature and other specimens led him to view the world differently from others. His studies showed the connections between all living things on the 'tangled bank of life.'" Kathryn Lasky lives in Massachusetts.

Matthew Trueman was raised in Italy but moved to the United States to attend art school. He is the illustrator of *Noah's Mittens*, *When the Chickens Went on Strike*, *Tony and the Pizza Champions*, and *A Picture for Marc*. Matthew Trueman lives in New Jersey.